April 15, 2000

Dear Joan,
I hope you
have a wonderful
birthday! This is
a book I edited, and
I thought you would
enjoy the poems.
Love,
Susan, Gene,
Nicole, & Angelina

love and scorn

love and scorn

NEW AND SELECTED POEMS

Carol Frost

TRIQUARTERLY BOOKS
NORTHWESTERN UNIVERSITY PRESS

EVANSTON, ILLINOIS

TriQuarterly Books
Northwestern University Press
Evanston, Illinois 60208-4210

Printed in the United States of America

ISBN 0-8101-5099-9 (paper)
ISBN 0-8101-5098-0 (cloth)

Library of Congress Cataloging-in-Publication Data

Frost, Carol, 1948–
    Love and scorn : new and selected poems / Carol Frost.
    p. cm.
    ISBN 0-8101-5098-0 (alk. paper)—ISBN 0-8101-5099-9 (pbk. : alk.
paper)
    I. Title.
PS3556.R596 L68 2000
811'.54—dc21
                                                            00-008057

The paper used in this publication meets the minimum requirements of the American
National Standard for Information Sciences—Permanence of Paper for Printed Library
Materials, ANSI Z39.48-1984.

To Dan and Susan

. . . come just before sunrise and see and taste again
the apple tree coming into fire

—shadow-glyphs on the crystallized grasses,
geese surging above the loblolly pine, the smell of sap—,

as if willingly through its long life
it held on to one unclarified passion and grew and regretted
  nothing.

O birds on easy wings,
lions, stags, leaping fallow deer,
mountains, valleys, shores
waters, winds, passions
and terror in the watchful nights.
—Saint John of the Cross

The world is a raving idiot. . . .
—D. H. Lawrence

Contents

New Poems

Abstractions

Selections

Acknowledgments

The poems in this volume were published in the following collections:

The Salt Lesson: "In Common Places," "The Potato Eaters," "The Salt Lesson"

Liar's Dice: "All Summer Long," "Liar's Dice," "The Undressing"

The Fearful Child: "Country Marriage," "The Day of the Body," "The Fearful Child," "The Haircut," "The Heron," "The New Dog: Variations on a Text by Jules Laforgue," "Ode to the Horseshoe Crab," "Winter Without Snow"

Day of the Body: "The Bride," "Carousel," "A Field Full of Black Cats," "Girl on a Scaffold," "Harriet Street," "Mallard," "Notes to the Cold," "Redbirds," "The Snake Skins," "To Kill a Deer," "The Tumored Angel," "Web-Making"

Chimera: "Alto," "Apology," "Apple Rind," "A Childhood Memory," "Chimera," "Eating the Whole," "Icarus in Winter," "Mozart," "Sunfish," "Wild Partridge," "Winter Poem"

Pure: "The Argument," "Art," "Away," "Balance," "Country," "Fate," "Fury," "Harm" (a much earlier version appeared as "Root" in *Chimera*), "Her Beauty," "Horror," "Laws," "Mind," "Music," "Nothing," "Papilio," "The Past," "Pure," "Recompense," "Secrecy," "Sexual Jealousy," "Thrill"

Venus and Don Juan: "Abstraction," "Adultery," "Comfort," "Companion Of," "Compatibility," "Conscience," "Crows," "Ecstasy," "Envy," "Homo Sapiens," "Imagination," "Joy," "Lies," "Pity," "Scorn," "Self," "Sex," "Untitled," "Venus & Don Juan"

The above poems originally appeared in *Antaeus, APR, Atlantic Monthly, Chariton Review, Chelsea, Colorado Review, Crazyhorse, Georgia Review, Gettysburg Review, Indiana Review, Iowa Review, Ironwood, Kenyon Review, Massachusetts Review, Missouri Review, Montana Review, New England Review, New York Times, North*

American Review, North Dakota Quarterly, Northwest Review, One Art, Partisan Review, Pequod, Pivot, Ploughshares, Poetry Miscellany, Poetry Northwest, Prairie Schooner, Quarterly West, Seneca Review, Southern Review, Tendril, TriQuarterly, Virginia Quarterly Review, Volt, and *West Branch.*

The uncollected poems appeared in the journals cited: "After Grave Illness" (*Kenyon Review*), "Burdock" (*Prairie Schooner*), "Egon Schiele's Wife" (*Shenandoah*), "Endlessness" (*New England Review*), "Flicker" (*Quarterly West*), "Fright" (*New England Review*), "A Good Night's Sleep" (*Kenyon Review*), "Komodo" (*Southern Review*), "Pear Tree" (*New England Review*), "Procedure" (*Kenyon Review*), "Red Pond" (*Kenyon Review*), "Robinson Crusoe's Hair" (*Massachusetts Review*), "Rural Weather" (*Kenyon Review*), "Sin" (*Ploughshares*), "Summer Canon" (*Kestrel*), "The St. Louis Zoo" (*New England Review*), "Thaw" (*TriQuarterly*), "The Torturer's Horse" (*Gettysburg Review*), "Waking" (*Kenyon Review*), "Youthful Venus" (*Gettysburg Review*).

Thanks to the editors.

love and scorn

new poems

Matins

I've felt undeserving. I've made myself ill with the glory,
in the unleavened garden
disgorged the lies and scared away with a stick a snake.
What made me covet that which I could not have?

I've grieved and walked in catacombs,
I've felt undeserving. I've made myself ill with the glory.
Even the falling leaves gesture their renunciation.
I disgorge the lies and abhor the serpent's hiss.

I remember seasons, things I bring from far away,
and grieve. I walk in catacombs.
In gardens now, by the stone walls, sunlight closes,
the falling leaves gesture their renunciation.

I remember being in a field touching a man's body.
I remember seasons, things I bring from far away
and things that hold their breath for shame.
His skin was soft as a girl's and he closed his eyes.

I placed apple petals on his eyelids;
we were lying in a field and I touched his body.
Then there were clouds, an uncanny silence,
as when in a green place the air holds its breath for shame.

What made me covet what I could not have?
Ill with the power and glory, a thrashing in my chest,
I remember the unleavened garden,
petals falling singly, the yellow snake disgorging lies.

II

I've grieved and walked in catacombs.
I've felt undeserving. I've made myself ill with the glory,
power and glory—
a thrashing in my rib cage.

I've gone into the unleavened spring garden,
disgorged the lies,
and scared away with a stick a snake.
I've grieved and walked in catacombs.

What made me covet that which I could not have?
I've felt undeserving. In this bright land
that changes from yellow to green and back to yellow,
I remember seasons, things I bring with me from far away

and things that hold their breath as if for shame.
I've made myself ill with the power and glory.
I've gone into the unleavened garden
and startled a yellow snake

disgorging lies. A thrashing in my rib cage.
What made me covet what I could not have?
I remember seasons. Things that hold their breath for shame.
Things I bring with me from far away.

III

I've made myself ill with the power and glory.
I've made myself ill with the power and glory.

Robinson Crusoe's Hair

Poor Robin Crusoe, where are you?
Where have you been?
How came you here?
—Poll

The lime tree, the eternal bars and bolts of the sea;
the marl cave; his compasses and books of navigation,

perspectives, dials; the great heats and no breeze;
the dog who could not talk to him; the parrot who sat on his finger

and laid his bill close to his face and did; barley; goatskin parasol;
three good Bibles; the principles of Nature;

the last uses of his ink to minute down the days
when strange things happened; the broken and imperfect prayers;

and when he was ill with fever, his hair—
chestnut like his father's—falling out, then growing back;

he felt the soft stubble at the temples;
he read Scriptures, hunted, preserved or cooked his kill, napped, built
        hedges,

and this gave him sometimes such covert joy; he rubbed
his fingertips lightly above his ears and behind where the two cords

of the neck run, and he could feel the hair multiply,
and it came in silvered and very curly, coarse almost

as the hair of coconuts:— All this balanced
against an earlier hardened despairing of dangers, and

once, as he rubbed back the new head of hair
in a torpor of distraction, the silent ceiling over silent sand,

he felt water squeeze from under his lids. And later when Friday
        stroked
his own father's face, fed him cakes and chafed his arms and legs, he
        cried again.

Songs for Two Seasons

After Grave Illness

The body has two seasons
and doesn't exist to be changed;
it itself changes—as a clearing fills
with moths, then into it steps the hunted deer.
Who knows from the outside
where death grows?

I rub my eyes as if to recover
some first sight. Clouds purple.
There is rain; there's snow;
a northerly wind crushing in its teeth
the year's seeds.
I am pushed inside
out like a glove showing its lining.
Things simply are.

Red Pond

How cool it lies. It only speaks
of having little feeling—or too much.
Drop by scarlet drop its rhetoric spreads

to the farthest shore, waters
dislodging the pebbles and roots. Who watches?
Who watches this ancient mirror loves
the wind's effacement and the querulous silence,

water because of the sun,
sun because of drifting stars,
stars because of the beautiful surface
and traces of red mud.

Marsyas's Art

When the god came with his lute and knife,
asking, Have you made your last song?—

I told him I would make him the song for death:
great light of light, air like juice edging

around a figure torn into small tents, circles,
knitted chain, gold. And the scorning flute.

Procedure

The flesh comes free and the nodes
are loosened from their element.
The nerve will never stir; no
caress again will cause a tingle.

Bandages pack the numb chest,
the eyes are only half
opening—half-wakened by the ebb
of drug tide.

Am I Gorgon, odd-
breasted, corrupt, I wonder. Bitter
complicity: The male nurse
nods and turns from me.

Youthful Venus

The sea foams and the ivory body
(modeled, painted) stands in the open palm
of a giant mollusk; the water yields, the waves are calm.

The eyes open suddenly and the ears, hearing a gull—
song of sails, of loneliness. Still,
her mind in half-light, lightward leaning.

She breathes air not water who inhaled
brine and deep so long. Is it true—
the world all beauty, sunlight and blue,

a single mast on the horizon?
No man near. Exhilarated with being born,
she swims leagues to the whispering shore,

her curled hair wreathed in colored beads
of spray. She is tired then; enough to delight
in lying in the sand. Sleeps. Dreams. The light

passes over her with thoughtless hands. Let her be.
Think of other daughters. Turn back your boat.
Think of black eyelashes pulled apart

suddenly and the extraordinary white of her eyes.
Stop your smile that she may know without disguise,
before the gleam of desire, overwhelming joy.

Paradise, Reentering

Delirium of the hot and sleepless nights
of August—

when the mind wanders
back to a gate, glow of all that fruit
that will not bruise, a woman or a man
running breathless at your call—

it reminds me of a tremendous rusting bridge,
crossed and recrossed, the red sky peeling.

Someone is seated on a bed looking back
at whoever stares in, smelling
of tobacco, sweat, the brine of sex.

Waking

It was dusk, the light hesitating
and a murmur in the wind, when the deer, exhausted,
turned to look at me, an arrow in its side.

Though I pity dreamers, taking a thread
and weaving it upon the loom of Self—the secret,
gaudy, wonderful new cloth—, I will tell the end of the story.

His shoulder was torn, the joint held by one sinew,
which I severed with the blade of the arrow,
so when he ran there were no impediments.

The black dogs that followed were swifter,
their barking ancient, despicable.

As he fell, his chest turned to breastplate,
his one powerful arm covered with pagan signs.

Nearly stupid in my waiting for what would happen next,
each breath propelling me and him toward dust,
I woke, the sheets soaked, heart fluttering—:

When death comes into the sleeping room as through a tiny hole,
like a rent in the Covenant, it hurts.

A Good Night's Sleep

Reassured that we return as before, we enter
a land where everything changes, densities, colors,
rhythms of breathing, and we meet the dead.

What sort of name might turn up inside our pockets
if we remained there? The hair stands on end.
The repose around the eyes can't wash off;
it only becomes a little cleaner.

And the ones we did not know we loved
we follow down the nights
in cities half-built of where we've been, half-
built of ribbons.

. . . the body itself divine and absent, the lineaments
of beauty stored even more powerfully in thought:
the ankle's pale butterfly in a chrysalis.

What would we know of this going-hence
but the occasional fissure of light?

Ai, the divine ignorance of closed eyes.

. . . missing only that moment of coming to,
as if giant hands extracted from a small rip in fate and placed you,
who counted for so little when liberated in sleep, where you last stood.

Rural Weather

The sun shaking open the pink and yellow sky—
lakes showing their early fires—has grown taciturn and withdrawn in
        Arkansas,
where a tornado, deeply out of its own depths, stirs.

That is *now,* and I am at my window a spring morning
imagining "later on" and "then" and "after that." My cat, delicate
        Satan,
walks from the garden with a vole dangling from his mouth and lays
        it by the back steps.
If I praise him, he will eat it. Or it will be left to rot.

And the young murderers on last night's news
went like angry angels through their parents' house (they could not
        bear them
any longer), as if to mock the eternal Coming.
No spirit seek rest here; the new squall soughs down the hillside.

Somewhere is it brighter, unpromised, unwritten?
. . . clouds leaning their swan necks in sky and lake water, light
        brimming after rain
in apple petals?

Burdock

In the April sun that doesn't yet smell, brown and red birds declaring
      hunger,
I appear from the inner world—a hell of beetles and voles—
      appointed to multiply.
If tender, I'm streamy with orange dye, used to the gardener's
      scritching hoe, rock-
rooted. Buried, lopped up, drowned, how can I be hurt, when I
      resurrect? I resurrect
at the sun's behest, my leaf liquors concentrating into bitter-meated
      flowers
and stiffening into stalks. When my eggs burr the coats of animals,
      who can neither mate
with me nor eat me, they take the future into the cold fields. I'm here
      in this late
morning, to tell you there is satisfaction, even when I die; there are
      grounds
and consequences. I am compact of laws, emerging continually from
      the inner world.

Pear Tree

As at the bottom of a mirror,
the quiet dregs of someone's late hour—
comb, jewels, a fist of silk—are,
the pear blossoms.

The heart must learn to go through the seasons
slowly, whose entrances are riddles.

One is a bower in a wood,
morningless, full of snowy shadows
and what inside of them calls to.

Another is the endless
river which no longer
longs for trout and salmon, its surface
bubbling with copulation.

Copulation, birth, death—:
the finches sing and rattle in the leaves,
blunt figures among the multitudinous buds
and incipient fruit.

And if in the ditch beside the pear tree I find
a quatrefoil of buttercup
and a deerhead
on its stripped spine like a keyboard from a dismantled piano—

the ruin and beauty—,
wood-nurtured,
my bag of dreams
empty, I will feel my niggardly heart
and go on.

The St. Louis Zoo

The isle is full of noises,
Sounds, and sweet air . . . sometimes voices.
—The Tempest

High, yellow, coiled, and weighting the branch like an odd piece of
      fruit, a snake slept
by the gate, in the serpent house. I walked around the paths hearing

hushed air, piecemeal remarks, and the hoarse voice of the keeper
      spreading cabbage
and pellets in the elephant compound—"Hungry, are you? There's a
      girl.

How's Pearl?" A clucking music, then silence again crept past me
on the waters of the duck pond. Birds with saffron wings in the flight
      cage

and flamingos the color of mangoes, even their webbed feet red-
      orange, made so
"by the algae they ingest," as angels are made of air—some bickered,

some were tongue-tied, some danced on one leg in the honeyed light.
I thought of autumn as leaves scattered down. Nearby, closed away

in his crude beginnings in a simulated rain forest, the gorilla pulled
      out handfuls
of grass, no Miranda to teach him to speak, though he was full of
      noises
and rank air after swallowing. Smooth rind and bearded husks lay
      about him.
His eyes were ingots when he looked at me.

In late-summer air thick with rose and lily, I felt the old malevolence;
the snake tonguing the air, as if to tell me of its dreaming:—birds of
    paradise

gemming a pond; the unspooling; soft comings on, soft, soft
gestures, twisted and surreptitious; the shock; the taste; the kingdom.

In something more than words, *You are the snake, snake coils in you,*
it said. Do you think anyone knows its own hunger as well as the
    snake?

Why am I not just someone alive? When did Spirit tear me
to see how void of blessing I was? The snake hesitated, tasting dusk's
    black honey,

to feel if it was still good. And through its swoon
it knew it. Leaf, lichen, the least refinements, and the perfection.

Komodo

The flight of a white cockatoo from tamarind to tamarind
still in his mind's eye, one morning, Baron von Biberegg lay down

like a streak of flowers in the dust. Lush mist, animal calls, & birds
       sinking, the mind
breeding without moving—O sleep, O golden hive. Then a giant
       lizard

appeared. When? Within an hour. In modern times.
As out of a dream's monstrous whirlpooling,

the monitor with flaming, olfactory tongue probing the air,
consumed the Baron—hands, ivory teeth and bones, skin and
       fabric—,

whose sap mounted in terror or disbelief, groaned, spilled, then sank
       into the ground,
the sun deranged in the fronds.

                  ⌒

To be utterly missing, given over like drying rain,
so that at some point his wife had to give up grieving,

his companions searching the bamboo groves, *tanah panas,* the
       unplumbed,
hot, estranging forests, then placing the white cross

to mark their last glimpse of him, and to tell themselves
he *had* been, his having-died filling them like abundance . . .

—wasn't he already a part of the dragon, visible in the yellow eyelids,
septic teeth, clawed feet solid as the bottoms of brass table legs?

Sentinel, snare, spirit, devourer, relative of the ascending bird.

⌒

And the Promethean feasting; the shaking of the fragile frame
through sunrise and day, the throbbings through nighttime.

No one there to see the mouth tremble or to hear his thoughts.
Soul winces—as though divinity *could* be drained from him.

Yet Prometheus, yet the risings and settings of the stars we know
to follow, yet all the instructive frenzy lives

leaf by leaf, step by step, in the brandishing moment
and in the way the mountains and the savannas are waiting—

as the mind waits, the startled little bees that leap below sense and
        unseen.
Also fragments of liver, spoiling in the air, propose defiance.

⌒

And the ones who study the monitor lizard, while deer lie
napping in the azyma bushes?— the ones for whom Orpheus's music

carries little sting or sweetness as they watch, in bird cry and tam-
        bourine
of sunlight, the lizards tongue the white fecal pellets of their rivals,
        and hold

the tongue and lashing tail in their hands for measurement? For them
neither heart nor devil nor god figure; no perfidy in the reptile's
        ambush; no metaphor;

only viscera, anatomy, the echoing straits between Indonesian islands,
        isolation and escape.
Lizards prowl, eat, and mate, trued by the tips of their tails.

They lie in the grass or in their holes, with head outside the mouth
of the burrow and eyes wide open, staring into the black surrounding
        forest.

If this is it, if they completely inhabit themselves, there are no morals
or excuses. None for the disemboweled, disembodied: goats, pigs,
        horses,
the blazing cockatoo, the pink, lightless, inner tissues of the Baron.

Thaw

Clouds brown in a puddle
                like the skies Job learned

to find beautiful; the fields
                chaste, yes, but far away

violet and blue-green trees
                on dawn's cold sleeve;

manger-rich, ah, sweet, the dirt;
                the music of melting

gathering head
                where blind fishes wait, cold

and unable to tell mercy
                from fathomless grace

in this presence, this absence,
                this cold presence.

Can the flawed heart fill?
                I saw in a flash of pain,

in a cold fever,
                all my Februaries

turn from winter, then turn again.
                What can I do

but move to and from my nature
                and call those moments

sweet that teach me
                to find in the drift of eastern gray

and cold western gray—

                in currents, spicules,

and feathers of snow, volleys

                of sunlight—that I am no longer

what I thought myself to be,

                even with the overwhelming regret

that comes with this joy,

                the simple assumption

that I may have to leave this place

                sooner than I want?

The Torturer's Horse

Though he painted the saint's body with reserve—
all in ruin—and the harsh blue thistle in the foreground,
he let the vista be large and multiform, a spring storm in one place,
people playing cards in another, peat bogs, swallows in a hazel tree,
a horse rubbing the great muscles of its rump against a post. Death
      small?
Only as a slit in the body's side may be cliché, and a bad artist
paint a ribbon of blood from it. Where another, looking
out his window, sees January, August, and November
absorbing the figures of townspeople, as they go along. He will sit
      before
his canvas in the early morning hours and paint the equine head,
hogged mane, and firm stance of the torturer's horse, like an irony
he just found out. And while dipping the brush in the brown paint,
feeling how all life and its labor are in his following the curves
of the hindquarters, he will smile. A ribbon of blood? A saint
lost in a mob? How marvelously sad. And incomplete.

Books

There was a mongrel and Dick and Jane.
They didn't make sense.
Alphabet in pieces; stumbling tongue, as if salted;
fingertip slowing the voice,
making the ear not err. A glimmer, finally,
so the sounds spelled a name,
naming the picture.
There they were by the *water*,
paper people and a dog
I'd have to go a long way around now
if I wanted to forget—
enchantment so strange it took some getting used to:
the runes and passwords,
Spot's *woof* which was Cerberus's,
witch house of icing, velvet forests of wrongs
and rights, Lost Boys, wooden Jonah, Marys,
sleeping in the dark leaves
while my cup of milk (tea or wine, later) grew tepid.
Learning how far my life reached,
and where emotion wakened,
I've felt over and over the sense of tumbling
through light- and anemone-strewn
oceans to the bottom
where I've lain like a slain thing yet breathed,
a body given over to quiet,
imagined creatures breeding in the shoals;
and only with great effort able to look up
if a sound (someone calling?) broke the surface;
then, as if it were trying hard to be spring,
a greener light, as though through a green window,
raising all that was saturated, magnified,
from those depths—saving it and storing it up inside:
the once and ever after—the *the end.*

Flicker

Beauty is for amateurs.
—William Matthews

Chisel-billed, eye cerulean, with a crimson nuchal patch,
flicker lay on the ground, still-warm, and went on aging:
intricate, stricken watch, pear in a desiccating wind.

I brought it home and began with the box of watercolors
to wash the eye with milk for the clouds and sky it fell from,
then dragged my partly dried brush over the rough paper surface

for true textures on the wings, imagining old orchards, umber and
     sienna,
where I'd seen the undulating flight of loose flocks. I studied
the yellow undertail, then daubed with the colored water

along the gray and dun stripes. As for my pulse, I felt for tempera-
     ment—
for gravestone, for shadow—to affect the utter silence after a long,
     long day
of call, *whurdle, peah,* drum, and *wicka.* Then I blotted and scraped
     the throat.

I saw dusk falling like a comment on each detail
that led to it and gradually was lost and leaving.
A hint of song must be caught, a clarity of neither light nor memory,

and it must be in the physical form of the flicker
and the orchard where the wind makes a soft racket—song that
     breaks the learned heart.

I stared and stared by lamplight, stroking the white,
thinking sour gum, dogwood, poison-ivy berry, river mist, imagining
     the free side of the hills,

when a bead of liquid formed in the flicker's beak and pooled on my
   desk.

My evasions went up in smoke. With colors, tones, casements,
and stars with exact names, who could but feign the moments
once lived that will never be lived again?

Who has a home in this good world and doesn't yearn?
I do. It's mine. I do.

Egon Schiele's Wife

More since her illness he tried to think of her not purely as wife—
as someone who finds herself trying to please, to
be of his mind.
                    The spread legs and bunched-up slip,
                        the reddened labia, and an almost compulsive
                            abandonment:
they were his wishes.

                            As for her—
sprawled like a goose sideways down the wind whenever he drew
        her sex—
what was enfevered began slowly to fade
and she was lost to him (you know how that feels?).

He drew her face, then gave her pen and paper
so that she might leave behind for him
love's avowals. In the weirdly devastated eyes
of the earlier self-portraits, where aloneness exaggerates everything,

he hadn't yet mourned yet almost seemed to know. . . .
                    Ah, she'd have gladly lingered
                        in that yellow and ocher room that willed and
                            willed and willed her,
for just a bit longer,
                    but found Death determined
and went with him, whose whispered secrets and stale fragrance
mingled with decay excited her. The artist stepped to the morning

window and looked at the quieted-down square. —A clearer
feeling now: the nude heart in ecclesiastical colors
above the city's grayness. Their erotic life.
And something more, exhaustion,
like halos in an unexpected gust of wind surrounding a tree's last
        leaves.

Summer Canon

When you leave me behind, leave me here
where fruit blossoms are thrown to the ground
in their season, and the watery pillars

of oak stand in the heart-shaped pond till it grows dark.
While you go, I'll wait for the deer to step
from dark brocade to sunlight in the clearing,

my life's work, my poems, no longer meant for you.
Finally alone, in a life too little my own,
I'll pick the wild jonquil and follow the wild deer.

After nightfall, the fallen ash, the bronzes
in the formal garden pulled down, I'll go home.
Say of me what you will, we are made such by love.

Sin

The tree bore the efflorescence of October apples
like the bush that burned with fire and was not consumed.

The wind blew in cold sweet gusts
and the burning taste of fresh snow came with the gradual dark

down through the goldenrod. The blue and scarlet sky
was gently losing its color,

as if from use.
The towers and telephone poles rose in the distance.

And a decline
of spirit, hearing, all senses; where the mind no longer rests,

dwells, intrigues; and Satan's quick perspective of what lies ahead
were foretold by the springing back of a bough.

—We'll never know the all of it: nature's manifesto,
the sleight-of-hand in god's light, the invisible,

visible, sinned against, absolved, no matter the enormity
of trying, and Eve's help.

But come just before sunrise and see and taste again
the apple tree coming into fire

—shadow-glyphs on the crystallized grasses,
geese surging above the loblolly pine, the smell of sap—,

as if willingly through its long life
it held on to one unclarified passion and grew and regretted nothing.

Autumn Tune

There, now you know losses
no one can give you back; and that harvests—
sugar of raw pulp—leave
a thirsty mouth. Fruit core and pips,

love, envy, unspoken regret
cruelly resurrect and you
know your limits. What will
you do? Remember

the light and vulgar tune
someone dead to you countless years
played one autumn. In slanting
light didn't you sway a little?

abstractions

Thrill

To say fabricated things, where freedom is forced
on young girls,
and give it your own sensual twist, pretending in their bodies'
natural curves lies a willingness like animals' to lick and rub each
       other
in the soft afternoon light. To thrill yourself with the imagined scent
of bodies redolent with oil and mango-colored.
And if a child's face releases a shadow,
no longer able to quiet herself with herself (*what,* for you, is wrong?),
to force her on to an ever deeper bliss—a nude queen lying on a
       green carpet,
a servant picking yellow fruit, and two old men near a large tree
discussing the Tree of Knowledge, your favorite scene.

Harm

She had only begun to get used to her body's exposures
to pain, like the insinuations behind questions: winter
asking the tree, where's your strength?— a priest asking a soul,
        where's your marrow?
Aversions, truth, invective,
it wasn't her answers which mattered, only her lying on a bed
being administered shocks until the world grew tired
of experimenting with another bit of clay and the inward liberties. So
        it seemed.
And when the intern came into the room, asking how she was
and snouting through her chest with drainage tubes, as strong a
        desire
as she'd ever had rose up in her. She must have gestured, or he
        already knew, because,
as if in expectation, he smiled at her and stepped out of harm's way,
        backward, for just a moment.

Pure

He saw that the white-tailed deer he shot was his son;
it filled his eyes, his chest, his head, and horribly it bent on him.
The rest of the hunting party found him hunkered down in the grass,
spattered like a butcher, holding the body as it kept growing colder in
      his arms.
They grasped his elbows, urging him to stand, but he couldn't. He
      screamed then
for Mary and Jesus, who came and were present. Unable to bear
his babbling, and that he might no longer have to be reproached, the
      men went to get help.
He only had left to him his pure hunter's sense, still clean under his
      skin,
a gun, the example of wounds, a shell's ease in the chamber, as he
      loaded,
the speed of the night chill, while his mind like a saint's tried to bear
that which God took from His own mind when he could not, not for
      another moment. . . .

Compatibility

Never after was life so filled with meeting,
with reuniting and drawing apart, as then, when bed-hot, filled with
      surges,
the man and woman began to know each other.
It was like the makeshift walking of geese toward water,—a settling
      into themselves and,
with a fiercer and fiercer grip, a testing of the untried other. How
      safe they'd been before
they touched and he asked her *one* thing which she meant to resist
      but was unable to.
How beautiful to keep one's fabled eyes closed:— Was another's body
      not like some bright
obstruction? But they, as if they knew nothing, opened entirely,
      bending to two wills,
striking down vanities, feeling what lay deep inside—the darker
      compatibilities—
until love seemed causal, not just related.
Their sinuous tongues used the word, over and over, without
      speaking.

Apology

Already the land is starting to forget gardens;
reminiscences no longer hold the heart completely
as someone held her a little roughly once in somber sweet groves,
and the touch she was utterly dissolute to, that caused collapse
        behind her knees,
sunslides in the lake, she feels a resistance toward, then apology,
as if a thorn catching her sweater has torn a small hole,—as if she
        shouldn't
have worn the sweater. What induces
then weakens the greater and lesser passions is what she'd like to
        know.
—Something like the green underneath red and yellow which is now
        wilting
has left her body; and she is someone who *had* loved
and is no longer availing and can neither take nor give away.

Scorn

She thought of no wilder delicacy than the starling eggs she fed him
        for breakfast,
and if he sat and ate like a farmhand and she hated him sometimes,
she knew it didn't matter: that whatever in the din of argument
was harshly spoken, something else was done, soothed and patted
        away.
When they were young the towering fierceness
of their differences had frightened her even as she longed for physical
        release.
Out of their mouths such curses; their hands huge, pointing, stabbing
        the air.
How had they *not* been wounded? And wounded they'd convalesced
        in the same rooms
and bed. When at last they knew everything without confiding—
        fears, stinks,
boiling hearts—they gave up themselves a little so that they might
        both love and scorn
each other, and they ate from each other's hands.

Sexual Jealousy

Think of the queen mole who is unequivocal,
exuding a scent to keep the other females neuter
and bringing forth the colony's only babies, hairless and pink in the
        dark
of her tunneled chamber. She may chew a pale something, a root,
find it tasteless, drop it for the dreary others to take away, then
        demand
more; she must suckle the young. Of course
they all hate her and are jealous of the attention given her
by her six bedmates. In their mutual dream she is dead and her urine
no longer arrests their maturing. As irises infallibly unfold,
one of their own will feel her sex grow quickest and greatest. As they
        dig
together, their snouts full of soil, they hope this and are ruthless in
        their waiting.

Envy

Look: the cat lifts its head, switching its tail, and to the other cat says
in a voice almost too low to hear, something angry, interrupting their
       shared meal.
Hissing, they both stand absolutely
still—quivering, full of mistrust—equally, it seems, over the bowl
       with its sweet morsels
of flesh, though one must start to feel the other's resolve greater than
       her own;
or the other fetches from within a hardness like a beautiful blade
from a locked cabinet; because the first breaks away and walks to the
       other side
of the room. While the other's eating recommences, she springs onto
       the pampered chair
and sits looking out the window at the birds flitting by, if cat eyes
       don't blur
at that distance, then suddenly turns her head down to her chest
in a burst of envy to lick and lick her own fur.

Laws

She knows of doom only what all women know,
deciding not to speak of it, since speech pretends
its course can be made to bend:—someone fleeing hot and sweating
and the victors close behind, then two roads all at once in a wood.
      Which one leads
farther away? Under cover of silence
she goes along as if perhaps nothing would happen to her,
seeming to be swayed by breezes—dazed, her friends say in their
      concern,
after, when they've thought of it, having called or dropped by.
Once, though, late in her illness, in the heat of a morning walk,
she raises her wig and shows us this surge of white back from the
      forehead. The tablets
Moses carried, with his guesses, in the end could not have been more
      blinding or more lawful.

Secrecy

It lay and dried in the sun, puffing, then losing its coherence,
and there was a sudden sickliness
in the air when the wind lifted and blew across to her, as if in
       ambush: cotton
and sweet chloroform. She ducked down and away, holding her
       breath, and went on
until she could sense no longer what wept and ran from the raft of
       skin.
It was as if someone had risen up, unwashed, bearded, from a copse,
and tried to come too near—with a gesture of supplication, knowing
that she was half-willing, tempted by strangeness (a bouquet
of lilacs in a beggar's hands)—and almost succeeded. But it grew
too intense, menacing. She shied. It was scarcely explainable
and could not be kept a secret. A branch lightened into place.
      Everywhere things decayed.

Nothing

She turned away. And her child slid toward
the ice edge of the precipice, gravity and momentum wrestling on his
    shoulders.
She could not bear to see the outcome and was starting to pretend he
    did not exist;
if his existence would come to an end. See: there is a snowy peak and
    clouds
spilling so softly they create a whirlpool of silence. She lets herself be
    in it.
She no longer hears anything. Not the wind. Not the scraping shoes.
    Not him.
How she used to fret, to brush the hair back from his eyes
so everyone could see his beauty and she could see the least shadow
of sorrow or illness. But there is nothing left to do for him.
Since the forces like acrobats keep somersaulting and playing
with him, she will not harken or give them the pleasure of her
    scream.

Art

Why when she gave her memory a mother whose cruelty was godly,
and who was beautiful, and the North African boy of twenty
in the Paris of her youth, who tore down
his fresco at the end of every day because the cement hardened
before he could paint his red angels—*Je ne sais quand,* he'd say—,
and memory *knew* she loved them, did it refuse to say so? She
        imagined she saw its gorge fall,
as after swallowing, and her own mouth felt like cotton.
She wanted to write it all down. What could tell her she would have
        to forget herself,
her art, everything, and make herself stare at a lake where a dragon-
        fly stared
at a tree, at nothing, then deposited its eggs in the still water and left,
as if it trusted or could go on without?

Imagination

Imagine that there are several paths. But none takes her
away. Whether she goes past the laid-up stones of the dam and a
        pent-up pond,
or into some foreign silent meadow with raspberry canes, she returns
        to the same
shaded entrance, as if she could never err, her mind won't let her.
Numbed and insane, she feels like someone's trapped stone
creature: a weather-beaten sylph holding on to a gate.
Why doesn't she just go, avoiding turns to the left and right,
until *everything* behind her is unfamiliar, unrelated; and she can be
        utterly new?
You may ask, but what do you know with your maps, books, and
        clocks? Stuck
as you are, will you yank off the silent dial face and, taking no
        counsel,
walk unfettered into the wild north fields?

Her Beauty

By now her beauty no longer catches glances like small animals in a
        gentle snare,
autumn having thinned the light and frozen its blossoms in the field.
Even her looks of imprecation and her frowns seem weak,
and she says fond, foolish things about herself,
about once having been greatly admired, envied, fated—
a Psyche to Venus—and how she loved her husband who was faceless
and gave her pleasure. Better than pretending
indifference—like the heaping snow;
better to say what she by another once had known,
only so secret and withdrawn the way it is in mornings,
in weather, an animal's fur bristling, a moleskin.

Fright

Dusk bled. For the frightened fledgling Silence's sake
it barely moved, the jugular going pale,
and gave no voice to world or dream or, sometimes like rose
      interiors,
worlds within a dream, our spilling desires.
Dusk released this surge. What to say? I can't seem to get past
      autumnals
and a scared sense of the abstract. I want what the borough dweller
by the Hudson, murmuring, and the land tiller want: that for
      unsayableness
(some beauty, some ruin) a falcon unfold its wings
with a shy solemnity and, coaxed, lighten its grip on the wrist
of the forest . . . radiance, unaccountable reds that ignite
small fires in water, and companionable motions of a mind, only
      just human.

Music

You are right. At death I might well desire both day and rest,
some calm place where light is stabilized on an arbor,
a table, green glasses, and damask. The taste is of earth and sunlight,
tomatoes with folds at the blossom end and a large rough navel
with a bit of stem still attached, oil with basil
and lots of garlic, causing thirst for wine. And the music
to be played at my funeral must be the sound of the rosined bow
working against the wind, not old keys that are only echoes, but
      strange
gold in the beetle's click, a jay, a three-color bird, a brown thrush,
their asides and intimations like the napkin songs
of great composers, written before the last bread and wine are gone.

Horror

When horror, that with pretty masks
no longer stood to one side as he walked from his house to the
    garden,
extolling neither the magic of the atmosphere nor his medals that he
    earned for painting,
but undefinable, still deferred—
as if somewhere a prophet had put down his hood and bellowed—,
grew colossal, Goya put fourteen black versions of it on his interior
    walls,
the most audacious a dog whose trespasses have sunk him in an
    abstract grave.
That he cannot go to the Master toward whom he is looking is in the
    slight blue stain
in the dog's eyes, that Goya wanted the whole room to see how
    terribly the dog wanted
to go is in the tipped yellow absence above his head. This is how it
    was and how it is: caught, wholly
tempted, without a clue. How little has art driven off.

Joy

Ah, that Noah's joy lasted only for a time presses itself on the heart
      and mind.
When they called him foolish, he went on building.
But then among the drowned like soaking marionettes the ark
      bobbed, so that even
his closest friend meant *nothing* to the Father:— How could he hold
      on to his beliefs?
Like the caged beasts roaring, and as the wind beat itself on the
      water and the hull,
wouldn't he have liked to ease himself with yelling? Suddenly it
      comes to you:
He did yell. The trust he'd flung out with such abandon was absorbed
      by the gray pall.
And you harden yourself against the appearance of the landbird
—as if sunning his anguish and walking in washed and earth-spiced
      air
could rid the nostrils of the stench of the past forty days—,
a consummation that makes the sweat grow cold.

Mind

As he went on—no one else in the yard, late, well past dinner—
        stacking cordwood,
it was as if his body, supple and allayed,
by sweat, were surrendering to something larger than itself,
        unpossessed
by moonlight, so that when from the shadows, head-
first, exhausted, August fell, he sensed it; it was neither the wind
nor the dark that so increased in all things they almost perished,
but more like a theater curtain drawn back—: There stepped
lives not completely lived,
yet inflamed, and a wooden staircase. Out of death and promises
        he'd made,
his mind, in rhythm with the lateness of the world,
that turning, saw absence and its presentiments step down, as if free.

Self

They left her alone; it was what she wanted.
The bay waters had not been so secret for a long while, their great
      labor quiet.
She rowed over the calm of the ebb to an island of birds—heron, cor-
      morant, egret waiting in the tall
mangroves, placid and self-contained, as if she alone were meant to
      see them
and find some meaning there. She back-watered through the down-
      strewn shallows
until one-by-one, then faster, all the birds rose, clucking, in some trib-
      al crescendo. Immense cloud
heads stood close, above, like the whitened manes of blind and vener-
      able gods,
gods, who remembering the fresh lands—now so remote—listened
      hard for the least shout
of anger or amazement. For a moment she felt she had pleased them,
though that hadn't been her intention, and no one else knew. But it
      remained in her:
what soared: the fierce rush: the birds crying fear: and herself the
      cause.

Sex

If, as with a flock of sexless sheep, gently and without craving,
        apparently,
they walk beside each other for days, not pressing,—only let either's
        depth stir
and the other wants to soothe and understand. With fingers, elbows,
        breastbones.
One has had one's anger, one's faction, one's guarded place
no one can get into, least of all one so close;
yet who would believe the almost lethal force one wants to strike
        with sometimes,
as beasts hurt each other, biting, clamping on to the wounded neck.
What is any more potent and familiar? Wasn't she the one in whom
many times the other lost himself without reserve? Can he be in any
        other person more?
If Venus can be of little further assistance to this *pair,*
when she surges through the one, the other is dragged there—was,
        and will not go away.

Fury

And the whole night she had told herself to be pleasant
as she lay by the sleeping man, and she'd gladly have listened to
    herself,
but as the enormous dawn sneaked into their darkness
and seized them in its paws, she found herself with the old fury,
past her carefullest politeness. She saw she'd need millennia to find a
    way
to comprehend the reason for the difference between their early
    ideals—
a garden where plums and peaches grew well and tasted wild
and they were unembarrassed by genitals—and what had become of
    them.
This apple-pose. It was no good blaming God or Adam, she knew,
    but she couldn't help herself—:
Why hadn't the one spoken forthrightly and had the other caved in?
Then, hardly allowing him to fully awaken, she said her first
    sarcasm. Then another.

Lies

Isn't there a race of people made of glass, who when spilling
too much of themselves on someone's sofa, in someone's house, act
       shattered?
They have come to the party as if in someone else's place,
perjuring with too-little-allowed and agreeable nods themselves:
When they laugh with the general laughter, it's a queer, ceramic
       chiming.
Who invited them? It's as if, wanting to fit in, they would give
       promise after promise,
limitless and indistinct, and as if they were their own diaries no one
       must read
except for a few paragraphs which contain a modest wording for
       what is not meaningless
nor all lies. On timid feet they carry themselves through the knots of
       men and women—;
every voice's tone is as if to be avoided, as if cold every other person's
       bearing—;
until one of their great sorrows falls from their lips. And then
       apology.

Recompense

That time, long practiced in pinning the alligator's jaw between his
    chin and chest,
the wrestler swam wearily, with long, blind hands and arms,
toward the brown eyeknobs, ignoring the crush and pester of the
    crowd
above the gator hole. And when the reptile bit,
he felt himself torn open, left exposed, accused—: fiercely,
that somehow a new existence could be formed out of the old. He
    remembers he rotated
with the alligator, attending to its muscularity,
pulling it down to the river bottom where its heart gave out and it
    drowned.
He tore the white belly skin for a belt. He took the stomach stones
as recompense for his disfigurement. —And all the while saving the
    crowd's glances,
which were tinged with respect, though some eyes wept and some
    looked at the darkening bayou.

Pity

When the woman falls in the garden and hurts her hand, all the
        blows
that have ever struck her, to which she had to yield, seem to return,
so morose the look in her eyes. But haven't they always been there,
saved up and partly concealed, so that she could look them over one
        by one,
eating and sleeping with them? The blows
live in her honeycombed mind and newly with each passing day
establish what she will give away and what she will share.
As she holds her wrist, she waits for the tumult in her body to
        dwindle—
a blue welt is forming under a fingernail—and she breathes the
        summer air,
soft as skin on warm tomatoes. It is hard to believe in what goes on
        without one.
And the heart learns a pity for itself, easy, coarse, common as the
        grave.

Adultery

Had she repented? Given over? No. She let others talk and pretended
to listen. It must be borne—commandment, moral—but not digested.
Jonah was not digested. And wasn't the inside of the snare sweet as
     ambergris some days?
She would not be another washed up on a shore, whose saving must
     be explained.
She would be with all the rest; for the rest: salt, tides, crying gulls,
     crabs,
the ones who catch crabs, the ones who kill those ones. These *were*
     her self,
and she would not purge herself. If her integrity was in question,
no one spoke of it, yet in company she was restrained, like one who
     in a moment
may say something coolly funny or devastating; until then holding a
     shell to her ear, to hear all
the singer hears, with hand pressed lightly to the ear—harmonies and
     the thrilling
unadulteration of her own notes, darkened perhaps with losses,
     sorrows, but still luring.

Abstraction

In the heart a paper copy of a daguerreotype is fading and the body
of the beloved is palest yellow, disappearing from sight.
O that I might once more hear you speak and refuse you,
making of myself the lover who is drawn no longer toward the loved.
But the years! The years are severed into mists no farewell can alter,
not even the farewell that doesn't look or sound hurt. "Love is the
        enemy of love,"
you said, knowing I could not feel your hands, your breath on my
        throat,
and not try to comprehend, speaking in the abstract and superlative.
And, "The moon forgets us every morning."
That's how it was: a dark uncircumvented cool ending,
and how it is, already no longer really linked to me.

Conscience

The crow settles on a fir bough and disappears
(the way an usher waits by the threshold to the Old Dutch Masters'
        room
and watches; what does he think?). Not even the hunters and the
        dogs
are reminders that the crow exists, and it would seem that he would
        never come back,
reuniting with others in the winter sky and moving off,
until he does. A caw falls like a reprimand from his beak, and he
        emerges in his uniform black,
his wings trembling stiffly with their free ends. It is hard not to feel
        anger
at his assertion—how one feels life's unfairness, and little to help us
        in our hard choices.
What use the silence, semblance, and austere flying?
As the deep woods tower above, full of shapes, and the heavens
        threaten snow,
something is moving near as if it wanted to tear us from our
        molds:—as a conscience is torn.

Balance

is how you carry it, how it is; for example, the turkeys which seemed
        ordinary—grazing through the
piled brush for butternuts, all head and feathers, then taking the shot
        because they didn't see you
standing on a stump,
one dying outright, the other baffled, half rising in the brown light
        and batted
to the ground—how ungainly large they made the afternoon, heaping
        up out of slopes,
trees, torn pieces of clouds
an excitement. When you stopped running, you took them from
        under your jacket,
where they had kept shifting and threatening to slip out,
still with a bit of warmth in them, and grasped one in each hand
by its horned feet like handles to steady yourself, leaning into the
land's steepness and accord, growing used to them, their difference.

Comfort

Because a sorrow was conquered, or a sin, can they relax?
No. Having felt hands crush and throw them down,
they see the ones in pieces everywhere and hear the eerie beat of their
       madness:
It trembles in the wings of hummingbirds, aloft as they eat, flying
       backward.
So they persist without knowing how, and having been forbidden
presence, to push and cajole the ones on their knees—in balls, in their
       and others' beds,
in hell—to their feet so that they can find a way for themselves out
       into an airy place.
There they take down the hands flung before the face
and help to wash the inflamed portions of the others' hearts, so much
       like their own,
invisibly anointing whomever they can with oils, until and when the
       soft
pounding of their blood becomes comforting—like being held again
       in someone's arms.

Endlessness

What's endless is full of death and joy
here, as with creation, light startling and unloosening
the water's surface, reflecting balconies, ever higher, we say,
and a foreignness of blue. The air ferments. Pairs of damselflies—no,
fours—circle, beckon, and touch tails, inside of which a small hand
      dwells
holding small jewels, proffering dynasties. They weaken
and fall. Imagine it were otherwise: a son from here,
outside fate, building a city of wood, supple, alive,
many-carated. Animals were things, and angels,
and flawless, as if from God's measure, a blueprint from a secret
      drawer. No
need for water for thirsty lips. Nor vinegar-gall.

Ecstasy

Her ecstasy rises like a rider on a leaping horse
and she knows to push through it calmly and completely, without
      rushing
or closing her eyes. The ground falls away, the sky, precipitate,
whirls about her shoulders, and she feels both saturated with motion
      and still.
If she thought (there is barely time), could it be of love's reciprocal
demands to give and be given?— as if an Angel appeared in the heart
and spoke: As your body rocks so shall his. So it seems,
because her hands, which were resting, dreamily
begin to stroke his neck and sides.
When she leans forward to whisper—a fondness and encouragement—
she is within herself again, exhilarated, and strangely proud.

Homo Sapiens

In this lonely, varying light of dawn with the residue of desire
like mist departing, I am walking. Was it in your eyes,
where my elongated face shone, I saw for the first time—
as if all the transparent fire in these trees had become palpable—
a hunger that was not wholly animal?
The need to tremble like dogwood, feeling the rain touch down.
My strange blood rises, and I may see you, fair leaves slipping over
       you, half-hidden
in the morning. With the beasts beside a pond,
I conjure the inward sun to leap into my brain. What remains?
Wild, beautiful petals all around.
A beast's face. And something, something else.

Fate

Imagine: in the twilight of a river, trout rising to the hairs and netted
        wings
of water walkers, and yourself casting a baited line
toward shadows. There is no talking, and the mind learns
to drift, to take in the slightest signs, as if there's already begun
under the surface what will come to pass; it lures you along.
Reed, ripple, raccoon scratches on the mud bank
lend their wisdom and their indifference to the moments before the
        pole bends double
or you give up, walk to the lighted house, and join the others at a
        table
to talk of life, love, logic and the senses, memory, promise, betrayal,
        character,
and fate—the driving notion
that around the river bend a magnificent fish waits, prickling the
        black water.

The Past

Was it in stepping into dusk? Did a glance release this turbulence
where Martin's fields thicken with thorn apple and a migratory bird
> makes
a sound?
Not even the quick flowering of April winds alters it, what a man in
> a straw hat
bending down
above the scythe's reach found, only now so saturated with rust and
> greatly indrawn,
the way it is in the past.
Yet the blade seems to will itself to hold an edge, expressing the kind
> of time
which plays around the roots of the grasses, and still knows, still
> passes,
still causes shadows
to seem to fit themselves around the ankles, refusing separation.

selections

All Summer Long

The dogs eat hoof slivers and lie under the porch.
A strand of human hair hangs strangely from a fruit tree
like a cry in the throat. The sky is clay for the child who is past
being tired, who wanders in waist-deep
grasses. Gnats rise in a vapor,
in a long mounting whine around her forehead and ears.

The sun is an indistinct moon. Frail sticks
of grass poke her ankles,
and a wet froth of spiders touches her legs
like wet fingers. The musk and smell
of air are as hot as the savory
terrible exhales from a tired horse.

The parents are sleeping all afternoon,
and no one explains the long uneasy afternoons.
She hears their combined breathing and swallowing
salivas, and sees their sides rising and falling
like the sides of horses in the hot pasture.

At evening a breeze dries and crumbles
the sky and the clouds float like undershirts
and cotton dresses on a clothesline. Horses
rock to their feet and race or graze.
Parents open their shutters and call
the lonely, happy child home.
The child who hates silences talks and talks
of cicadas and the manes of horses.

Alto

The day of chorus when she was sent out
for singing wrong notes, for conceiving
herself a soprano, she stood in the hallway.
Behind the door voices braided Bartók
into garlands. She had never been so ashamed.
See the roses, blooming yonder,
far from dead leaves—she heard the words
and saw the soprano notes perched breathlessly
above the staff, the red and orange vapors
making melody. She'd sung with the tenors
when they had the melody.
                              But now
she told herself this would be her lesson.
Outside the chorus room, the bottom
of the music brought her back, the darker voices,
she thought, like shadows in the song.
And though she listened for the unisons
as if for the meaning of a garden of roses,
when she went back into the room, the air
was filled only with the stale essence of their breath.

Apple Rind

Someone else was afraid and spoke to me
and I couldn't answer . . . swallowing oxygen
from a tube. And then? The cool blade
freeing rind from an apple
like the first touch of day. How long
I'd been in someone's still life—the blade
hidden, dividing—and was helpless.

Perfectly drugged, I lay just shy of winter
in my own mind. My cut chest felt nothing,
no terror, no pain. And there were morphine's sweet-
and-fruit boxes piled on the white terrain
like reasons for lives and death.
The orchard was weathered to admonitory bareness
except for a few frozen apples
above a disturbance of snow—the hoofprints
of deer coming by several routes to this late harvest,
the dim haunches and various limbs
afloat on movement that can break
or double back into the gray calm of woods.

How to explain directions a mind takes
or why I told no one how much I wanted
to come back to this beautiful, stupid world.

The Argument

Here is the cold, strict cell of the terrorist.
He is sorting through pieces of metal.
In front of him a pipe, wires, detonator, and a clock:
premises to follow through to the end.

If from an open bedroom door upstairs
a whimper or a sigh comes, he listens
until silence develops again, then turns
to the pile of shrapnel and pours it into the pipe.

Angels elbowing each other off the head of a pin
are not more violently correct,
nor more delicate, as he connects each part,
thinking, perhaps, of how the entrails and heart

are the House his declarations will be made in.
He has already scanned the newspaper for the date and time,
and he knows his victim's movements.
This is what I meant, what I meant

all along, you idiots, he says with his careful hands.
Why can't you understand
right and wrong aren't wired to the same clock?
Not today. Not now. Not my clock.

Then he sets the timer and lays the bomb in its cardboard tomb,
seals it, his saliva on the stamps,
and sends it to me, to you.
No chance to demur or turn leftist or wear a new swastika.
Not when he's finished and turned off the lamp.

Away

I

Their breasts and abdomens filled with air,
	grayleg geese soar on thermals,
between god's feet and hair.

The autumn light is silver and rose, foreign,
	and their flight is like some distant,
almost invisible allegory of what has gone

out of a person's life,
	less like the dying away of a chord
than a handful of pomegranate seeds, and Perseph-

one. The bodies of geese are light,
	the bones porous, hollowed to extreme thinness,
built exactly right

for leaving the gravel bed, and I imagine
	their tender, lazy lack of heart
as the trees rage into another season.

II

Just as the spring, which somehow begins
	and is nowhere, changes, or a hand
which reaches for an unexpected reason

and doesn't take my hand, not yet,
	so the somewhere that lies beyond me
becomes a disfigured garden, cold and wet,

yet not all there. It's as if it longed for me,
	or not for me. I heard voices, tender, primal,
speak to me, sing to me,

and remain a sorrow. And the hot
    air one September slathered my back and shoulders
with wax so that the colored leaves caught

there like feathers. Lightly,
    as after death, I imagine myself in skies past this one,
for there's no one anyplace who isn't secretly

going away.

The Bride

Gustav Klimt died in 1918 after a stroke, leaving his last painting on its easel, its principal figure half nude.

On a day snow flicks and swirls
and the Danube lies like a great silver fish
the wind and waves can no longer jostle,
Klimt lies paralyzed as if the bare space in the hospital room
has let its weight down on his chest.
Soon he begins to see in the white-slaked walls
a subtle, almost graffito flower fill
and a woman unlike anyone he has ever met—the thigh,
the naked foot, and the stirred-up mists
of her shoulders and face. He thinks of his painting
The Bride and how beneath the scrolls and orange flowers
with their sconces full of sap, the hairs of his brush
caressed the girl. He'd begun to fill in the anatomy
of her skirt, stippling the fallen petals and the pollen
upon the baroque cloth to wrap her nude legs and pubis.
Smiling, he thinks of his lover Emilie in summer,
her surprise when she raised the well bucket
and found a salamander bobbing there, and how a garden
is rhythmically absorbed into a figure of a woman
in the sun. He closes his eyes to imagine
the rouged faces and pale translucency of breast
and limb entangled in ornate silks near the girl
whose unfinished face makes the beholder more aware
they are parts of her dream which swirl in space,
in color, just below the surface of her thought.
Klimt tries to sit up. He looks at the winter bouquet
of flowers on his bedstand. Tomorrow he'll color
the apparatus and light of these blossoms
on the girl's skin with the brush's very tip, he thinks,
taking his time so not to wake her in her dreamt garden
until all the ovals, spirals, swirls, and triangles

tipped on their heads are worthy of a bride's reverie.
Only then will he know which qualities of her eyes,
smoky green with morning and rain or heavily lidded
as though from pollen, to bring to life. The woman
in the purity of the white wall waits, or seems to,
like a bride. Klimt wants her to dress and to remain
as if in a ceremony of sunlight, but reminded of her nakedness,
the marriage bed's, as he by gaslight on stone
and by the snow is aware of the bitter ease of the grave
beneath a bed of flowers. The next time he closes his eyes
he feels the earth open for him—the dark ajar,
the soil spangled with gold, an inert, unmoving flame—
and then a huge body, a blackness, has hold of him.

Carousel

A chestnut gelding and a rider balancing,
the blossom-smells, manure, late summer,
and the wooden ring they ride in—
I remember this and the weightless hands
at the horse's neck, impelling
the horse to canter, horse and rider
carving a circle in the dirt and air,
the stride and matched bearing becoming metaphor
for a carousel, gilt and red, forever
turning, as the hands are metaphor
for the still heart's wings, except
the horse's head tossed,
except they wheeled and suddenly leapt
over a cross-rail, trespassing
the dust that eventually must settle
on rump and riding hat,
leapt like pursuers after the sun
just cresting the morning
hills, leapt like my heart on some days
when I see made muscular and simple
the harmony and breaking down
of such harmony that is the passing world.

A Childhood Memory

A smoky autumn afternoon,
overcast. The children
have knives in their hands.
They are clashing quietly,

carefully, against the day's softness.
It is in the playroom. Cain's
forehead is unmarred.
Their bodies are light with feints,

jokes, and pride. The moments
simply pass through the room.
The father comes down the stairs.
He is in his bathrobe,

unshaved. He bellows,
his face creeping with the anger
in the house. For he doesn't know
what they do. What should they be without

the fight where they see themselves,
one running, one prone in a red stain?
The children have knives in their hands,
giggling, looking away from the man.

Chimera

By the verge of the sea a man finds a gelatinous creature,
parching, thick as a shoe, its head a doubtful dark green
that leans toward him as he bends near in some dark
wonderment of his own. The sky is haunted by pure light,

the sea a rough mixture of blue, and green, and black. Suddenly
he hears the air rent with loud cries and looks to see
pelicans on the piers raising their wings then falling, changing shape
to dive into the sea. He thinks of Bosch's rebellious angels
changing shape as they are pursued out of the immaculate sky.

Who are they? Angels who accept the hideous
and monstrous. Fallen, they make up a nightmare fauna.
Say the sea is to be questioned. Below the bounds
of this estate, through rainbowed cold, the rockheaded and cored

of bone, the chimera our madness does not cease to reinvent
and which we dare not think alive, crawls in a thick ooze.
Yet even this one, torn to the plain insides and leaking dyes,
exudes a gentle unrest of the soul. Is it not good? The man pauses,
looks around—the sea undulated, sharpening and smoothing

all the grooves that history has graven on the sand—
then he puts his hands under the terrible flesh and heaves it
as far as he can back into the Atlantic, as if it were the mirror
of a lost estate, the dawn-time of the world's first season.

Companion Of

And yet this great wink of eternity
—Hart Crane

October was what it had already become when I entered the walled
 graveyard, the air golden and remote
in the last minutes before evening. A bedstand and springs made the
 gate, pulled aside,
and the stones faced the sunset, all those which were not overturned,
 flung like cards
from the losing player's hand. How long the dead had lain listening,
 looking back,
was written on their markers—granite, sandstone, slate—also mar-
 riages, loves ("COMPANION OF")
homely avowals of affection cut in verse.
As day relented, I could have sworn there was no more reason for
 agony or joy,
that it had been outlived, except I saw one stone with the barest
 evidence of lettering—a staff with its notes
unsounded, but felt. And I knelt to make out what I could and ran
 my hand as if over paper over the cool stone.
And I found under a cache of yellow, crumbling leaves the pried-off
 surface, broken by the years
into nine uneven pieces. What else was I meant to do for Mary Hyatt
 but take home the words for her?
Then it was impossible not to imagine her days and nights, especially
 her nights, when the air seems to suffer most
from all that has come and what is no longer likely to come. She
 enters the rooms I lend her,
humming a melody whose words she's nearly forgotten. How signifi-
 cant and strange the badly remembered air.
It gets in her blood, no forget-me-not gayer for the neck and face,
 and the absent lover is everywhere,
in the shadows, frost on the panes, a soliloquy over the piano or the
 card game.
Before bed, she writes him a letter.

The last time we met you had less and less to say, and though I
  felt I understood
your private musings (oh, joys, memories of past experiences
  altogether your own
ghosts, guilts, pains), I felt my own words falling away from me.
  One quiet bred
another. In the end, we forgot to say good-bye. Tell me next time
  we meet you'll
read to me the lines of poetry you are so fond of, that I once
  heard you say with all
the passion of youth, that so moved us both, though we are no
  longer young?
Without the trouble of saying a thing meant, the meaning comes
  into suspicion.
And if nothing is meant, the thing isn't worth recall. I think I
  know your thoughts,
but isn't it better to hear them from your mouth? I long for you.

He responds, and everything is as it was. Her cheeks burn and her
  hands tremble.
  For years.
Until chance, seedy and blind, ruins them; in the fresh dark there are
  no words left
  for this. It is better so.
Worse to hear it from human lips than in the clattering leaves—a
  rancid song—or
  in the night owl's scream.

Country

Tables, chairs, a used refrigerator in a thicket
Of zinnias; a woman lifting a window blind;
A man crippled with fat who waves hello,
His dog on a short chain prowling in front
Of his angry shed, the fur unkempt and bearding,
Fervent as Rasputin to wrench free
And get to a new voice and a stranger's scent,
The garden primeval
With snails, wrung with yesterday's rain;

And the tire gardens, the pink and yellow rubber
Ringing the geraniums; the established names on the mailboxes
And gravestones weathering the rich light;
And the smell of old lilacs; the tin advertisements
For farm machinery rusting on the milk houses;
The lines of light between planks
Crookedly spaced; wasps' nests; starlings';
The surveyor's orange flags; the wrecked autos
Like specialty stores in a fenced lot;

And the auction block, the brisk rhythm
Of selling—going, gone—it is a journey
They no longer can keep ahead of, as under a tent
A revivalist and congregation melt
Into one large droning; or it is a big top,
The women tidying the trailers, tidying the junk,
With *Lonesome Road* on the radio, the men drinking beer
Around the clock, revving their engines,
And the mutt at leash end crashing left and right.

Country Marriage

They married out of school
when she could feel the baby's feet
fixed deep inside and feel
her passion quicken for the sweet

romance. He bought on time
a trailer on an ugly hill
and worked in town sometimes.
She leaned her forehead on the sill

and watched him tune the car
and vowed she cared for living things.
She saw how everywhere
the pollen cast its nets and strong

buds splashed a little color
onto the waving greenery,
then didn't mind the squalor
of axles, oil pans, grease, and flies.

She loved the honeysuckle,
the running light across the land;
she made herself a necklet
and spoke to him in tones of lead.

A quick in time, a bead
of blood, and dumb imaginings
became their solitude.
The yard filled up with junk and rings

of rainbow in the ditch
they got their drinking water from.
She didn't care so much.
She didn't care if he stayed home.

When summer turned to ash
a little witless sheep was born,
child slow to be itself
which lay in a crib all alone

caught up in their neglect.
She saw the bitter apple tree
and gutted car perfect
in winterfall, and senselessly

an equilibrium
held them something like love that year.
The child held in its arm
a sour doll. They had come far.

Crows

Not disputing what those nearest her would think, their questions
     and importunings, she goes out just after sunrise
into the morning green of the grassy earth, her nightgown soft
     around her legs, the gun cradled lightly across her forearms.
The crows which have waked her lure her along—darkly a solitary
     shape flaring through the naves of alder and beech,
the others calling. Those who have disturbed her sleep all month she
     means to kill, for sleep is sacred, and private.
She has only to think this and she will return home, barefooted, and
     climb back into bed.
The newspaper has not yet been delivered with its news of the world,
     the words chanting violence and death, violence
in the face of disappointment, violence for no sake, and in her pure
     daze her thoughts are more like this:
how far life reaches and where night and morning meet. From the
     mist a deer walks suddenly into her field of vision,
and as suddenly she fetches from behind blinking lids a hardness,
     raising the .22 to her shoulder and shooting it in the
     shoulder.
It falls, but when she leans into that remoteness—brown and still, its
     legs in the air—it rolls to the right and springs away.
There is on her now what she can know only by violence. She can
     smell it (fur, warmed earth grass, blood) and hear it
in the raspings of the crows as she tries to follow the wounded
     buck:—what has reposed all along in the part of her that
     isn't and is beast.

The Day of the Body

I. If a Model

If a model is posed by a sunny window
and the artist is in love with light,
he draws the white white vitals
of her body in sweeping unbroken curves
as if she were made of threads,
but if the artist is in love with flesh
and wishes to remain chaste,
she possesses for him all her animal beauty
in a belly and hips that are lit
as if by wingfuls of warm air
a day-sparrow caught in the sheaves.

II. She Thinks of Love

Wanting to suggest a wild and luxuriant soul
and her dignity, she molds her body
after Eve's. She sees herself
by a shaded brook; a dark purple road
and green foreground, where she
undresses. She looks at her belly,
then presses there with her hand open
until she can press no more,
and the ridges of fatty tissue
between her fingers are just fat enough.
Then, like Eve, she puts on
her lips an ironic smile
and lies down and thinks of love
which means of someone she has seen.

III. The Man and the Woman

The man and the woman
have been getting to know each other,

and now they are going to make love.
The bed represents the unlighted parts
of a picture, and their desire
seems to act as a wandering beam of light
that weaves around their thighs.
His hand defines the turning of her hips
just as her hips make his hands
their reality. Whether like tree trunks
or earth or light-filled air,
their bodies are caught up in a feeling
they do not quite understand: four dark
eyes surprised by each other in a room.

IV. *So When He Leaves*

They aren't violent, so when he leaves
in the middle of the night
he says, Tomorrow will be
like any other morning. He leaves her
lying on a light chrome-yellow sheet
only slightly indecent, as if she's bathed
in lamplight. After falling asleep
she sees a native girl on her belly,
showing a portion of her frightened face.
The background is purple,
a color of terror, but in the dream
she cannot tell what the girl is afraid of.
Perhaps she is thinking of someone dead
or that death is thinking of her.

V. *Where Are You Going?*

The looser his skin gets,
the more he gets used to his soul
flying in a frequently squalid room
like a bird. All the windows are closed,
and he is the child who ducks
each time the bird whirs by. With every fiber
the child wants to free the sparrow,
there is strain around his eyes;

but it will not light, and to the boy
the bird is unpredictable, may change
its circular flight, and crash into his head.
Sooner or later the boy will be brave
and rush to the door and open it.
"Where are you going?" the boy will call,
and the bird may sing, but no answer.
The boy will become a white dot
in a field, and the bird a vapor.

Eating the Whole

mouse, first the cat sits off to one side,
perhaps reliving the crawl into deep grass
and snap of the neck. A spinning leaf

mesmerizes him. How it tastes,
the skull he crushes, and what
shared images of stealth are released

at that moment, I'd like to ask.
He softens each part with his teeth,
then swallows all, the soft fur and red

sinew holding together like a piece of clothing
in the mud. What use to say
that he washes his face with his paws

and that he looks beautifully
insolent? In the shiny spring air
he stretches in a spot of sunlight,

pricking his ears for the birds'
exciting minors, drowsing, not a mouse-
hair on the lawn, nor a guilty murmur.

The Fearful Child

As a child I parleyed with animals, stuffed and real.
Making my kitten pilot of a boot, I guided
from one end of a string the dizzy flight and collapse.
I was fearful of people as well as things,
and my faithful toy shepherd with his painted face
sat by me on the bed in the gloom.
I was disdainful of dolls as weak people.

In the favorite story I told myself my parents
were made over into fair-limbed, brave angels
who smiled into their god's eyes when summoned.
I was benevolent, afraid to let go of this image
at night because I couldn't hide deep enough
under the covers to be overlooked by death,
the angel bending over me who had been wronged.

I read histories of queens, regal and barbarian,
whose leopard's eyes restrained man or wild beast.
I rambled along tidal rivers and in the marshes
where the green-golden grasses dazzled the sun,
and felt the ache of sea-air in my lungs.
I saw water spume near Atlantic cliffs.
I examined lichen. I saw great light drown darkness.

Then at thirteen I lay in the bleak bed before sleep
and heard the pleadings and the murderous kisses;
and burned, like a bear his fat, my soul.
I quaked at the sound of my voice whispering, *No,*
or turned my face to the wall
and wept salt onto my knuckles.

In the serene light of sun-up, before sparrows
tumbled up from the earth, whispering and singing,
and the exquisite sea and sky mobilized
their heavy, blue currents, I was consoled.
I walked through beauty without knowing why
and told no one, wanting nothing else to touch me
and never to move anyone in any way.

I hid away from the house and learned the dark
was not a dream but could show the pale gravel
of a real driveway. I saw for the first time
later the new moon and the full moon
in one piece. I no longer feared the night,
night like a bear at ease in his wide habitat.
In the greatness of such space I said, *This is me.*

A Field Full of Black Cats

Cats in fields sit
still as idols
catching sunlight
catching moles.

Through the broken lattice-
work of grasses
they stare for hours, black
pelts burning.

One can imagine
in the belly
of each cat's shadow
a mole being

held in thrall, completely
taking sun down
to earth, making
new terrain:

skies muscadine,
grass like tongues,
stones coughed-up
balls of fur.

Death is irremediable
here. There is no
reaching into the heart
of violence

when cat paws sweep
suddenly toward
the mole. The onyx
and yellow eyes

take the uptwisted flower
in as nothing
when cats walk back
to porches

to lick themselves and drowse,
the hunched-up moles
having ended
in their hot mouths.

Girl on a Scaffold

Her neck in a noose, the girl stands
on a scaffold with two officers and her lover.
She looks at the pale orchard or twilight
or the limb where a bobwhite's whistle
seems to originate. Whether the others hear
this fluting ahead of the wind can't be said
by the look on the girl's face.
The officer who is tightening the thick cord
watches the girl's brown eyes blink
several times and admires her courage
as well as her eyes which are brown as burnt loaves
of bread. Her neck is long and white,
and for a moment he wishes he could release her,
lift her into his arms and forget
how this day will end, but as he dreams
of their embrace on cool sheets, he sees himself
encircling her neck with his own rough hands
and realizes he has twisted the knot
at her tender nape too tightly.
As for the lover, he is no coward but
his throat is strangled and he is afraid
he will make a noise when she dies,
so he begins to hum a patriotic song,
the song stammering him; his hands are tied.
The other officer slaps him, and that is when
the bobwhite flies up where there was a knob
at the end of an apple bough. The bird
seems to blossom in the dying light,
and the girl's craned head lolls to one side.
With eyes shut she sees the hand grenade
leave the partisan's hand, then the colonel
leaning against the baked earth wall
putting on his socks. He was smiling
as if he knew how simple life is. Within her now
a feeling rises like the soft clashing of wings

to be free of red clay and the world twisted
by intent. Barefaced, in a soiled dress,
she stands on the trap door, heels together,
and listens for the last note of the bobwhite,
as if it were her dignity she strained for.
Shadows drain from the orchard
and gather at the base of the scaffold
as if a crowd of vague angels
has come to watch her fall.

The Haircut

When the boy's head is heavy with his own secret
cap of hair, his mother calls him to her
asking him to tell her about his day.
When last she called him from the depths
of the wood and combed with slender fingers
the golden current of his hair, the white
of his hidden brow, like a headstone,
had made her almost cry.
After she cut his hair, his head was quick
as a deer turning in a field to face new danger.
By the light raining down in a field in August's waste,
by the antique vase about to be knocked over
by his child's elbow, by her own perfume
lasting in the room after they leave,
can she explain her pity for him,
his forehead full of blond mysteries?

Harriet Street

The fadedness of stone
markers shows the wear
of weather. And here,
long life near a yard of bone.

She's naked and weeds
her garden, and seems to stare at nothing.
The hot wind swings
its sharpened sickle where dark deeds

jumble with good, and begun
things end. The wing a vandal
lopped off from a stone angel
props itself on her porch in the sun.

This bears deep looking into,
all the appearances of madness
and death, or is it just coincidence,
the ancient crone, not dressed, the few

artifacts of grief
strewn on Harriet Street
across from the cemetery? In this heat
perfect connections of belief

come easily. But look.
All her dresses blow
on a clothesline. She may not bow
to earth from burdens, but to pluck

what spasms of flowers
and gems there are,
most sweet, most stolen, where
near to the living, graves are.

The Heron

A woman and her children are on a lake.
The woman steadies a rowboat
by bracing her legs against the bulkheads
and with the oars that are like extensions
of her arms, as if there were no boat
and she stood in twenty feet of water.
Each time one of her children jumps off,
she is rocked back a few feet.
The lake's shades of blue are interlarded
with cool whites and greens, but the woman's eyes
instead of reflecting the water
are as clearly blue as the open air,
as if she sees without shadows,
her gaze quiet and reaching as a formation
of birds. And when the younger child
says that she is too far away, she scolds him,
saying she will never leave him
alone out there, that all he has to do
is flutter-kick a little stronger. That evening,
on shore, his face small and white
like the ivory back of a hand mirror,
he asks her outside to see the blue heron.
They watch it descend in slow spirals
until they must imagine its flight,
which might seem to him like a drawn-out
song of parting, each level a lower note,
the last a small white finale of water,
and to her a darkening hunt
for fish and frogs. It depends on her look.
Nothing else will tell him.
She wants to stay there and not break
the silence, not look like anything
until he answers his own questions,

like taking himself in his own arms,
remembering a time so solid
he could stand in the dissolving
day we know no more of than going.

Icarus in Winter

If Brueghel was wrong, and Icarus fell in the dead of the year,
freezing in the stratosphere that made his wings' wax brittle,
he fell here where a ball of suet hangs from a string

like a little low earth. How lonesome evening seems,
as if something felt part of itself missing.

The people indoors watching television, sitting in chairs,
seem never to come into the yard; they do not lament
the season's decrease. They only feed the few birds.

Where are yesterday's sparrows and wrens?
Above the branches of the oak,
washed in colors we feel but cannot find?

Swan colored, ice colored, rare-gas-and-light colored,
sounding to those indoors like a natural disaster—
a broken bough, a barn roof lost—Icarus

fell in this bare yard with no witness—no one
plowing a field, no ship of state concerned with itself,
no evidence of suffering.

                              These sightless walls
and shoveled entrances where no one comes,
even the white ground where Icarus is lying—

how sorrowless they make the landscape seem.
But no lie is made up entirely of lies,
and who knows who feels what and how much,

sickening at spectacle, turning off the TV.
Beneath the snow are pieces of every summer, buds and
stunted roots so far below sense that they don't show.

In Common Places

Wish I had been alone, your tread was a heavy cord
around my knees. Though we had come in a friendly way,
the need to tremble like a lake feeling the geese flock rise,
and stopped by your form, was changing me to sump.

I breathed the air from my neck and held still,
your arm a wall around me. Me over my head
to say the birds were strangely beautiful.
It's not that you haven't seen a miracle,

the heart of the world. I cannot look at you,
but as we trek and haul ourselves up this hill
you may be shivering inside, your eyes on fire.
A lover swooning with your rare voice tied.

We hold and take our secrets like a sad man
with his mistress. In common places. A country lake,
the moon an animal torch, a cheap, gray hotel room.
But when we quiver, we quiver deep and harder.

Liar's Dice

Used to mark a corner, a claim,
these totem rocks are painted into faces,
men. I have this stamp of land
with creeping jenny, jack-in-the-pulpit,
fir trees, and deep grass
I would not sell in a famine.

One way of ownership
is not to tell how much you have.
Liar's dice, the number of birds' bones
and thighs of foxes that click
on the table of the field I hold.
The checkered wind.
                              The gamble to sleep
with him when someone walking
with the cool moon or in broad day
may walk into our outdoor room
and fall on us like police.

Stood like a grizzly, emblem mask
to warn away intruders, the pole reminds.
I hide and shape my place,
own each pebble, use it all.
The beautiful fish, the warm birds.
Even if shown, love, they don't know.

Mallard

I raked up a mallard in the garden,
its body rolled in dirt.
It was as though I dragged
from its molded hill a large tuber
with eyes and buds for growth.
A horsefly landed on my leg
and a stink filled my nostrils.
The whole garden, dirt and air,
gave way to the death, as a birdflock,
thick at the center and jagged at the edges,
with a slight but irresistible movement,
veer south above a stubble field
or the sun enters the world.
The black feathers coruscated,
the garden was driven black,
and the breast went up
like the breaths of the just-born
or the sweet howling of the dog
that buried it.

Mozart

The books say genius, prodigy.
This means so little. Or that he loved his canary
perched on the wire swing
to sing

its repertoire of linking trills.
It's not the music he wasn't to write, nor the still-
unspent longings that led
him to his deathbed

singing his Requiem, nor the pauper grave;
but when he put notes and staves
on music paper
an aria or a prayer,

the softly boiling flames of spirit
that seem insubstantial, though we hear it,
were also caught there.
That he was here

at all, we fail to make sense of—
his trouble with women, his difficult love
for his father, his debts,
his death-

mask crumbling—except when we hear
his bits of song making architecture.
It's as though
a rococo

aviary were being built, with one bird
in mind, and it is liquid gold,
the intricate curving
bars proving

the singer is both held and free.
Such is his voice: a gust of melody
no one has known, flying yellow archangels
though all else falls.

The New Dog: Variations on a Text by Jules Laforgue

I

The new dog's sugary breath warms my neck,
milkflecks on his muzzle.
Day begins, lighting his lavender eyes.
Relaxed as a child, he seems to look
out across the yard at the sun's ascent.

The hour of last dreams when the bare elm
is tinged with gold. With this dog Max
I look out across the yard. I think
of newborn everywhere.
I think of Max who will wander
with curiously human eyes in the roses;
then imagine myself coming out of the garden,
going in place of Max to the road
and walking under a car.

I imagine entering this grave:
the full weight of Max counterpoised against
the glance he turned away.

II

You shovel the graveyard dirt too far
as if it were obscene to dig
a hole for Max, who is lying there
beside the rose bower, his ribs
and heart unstirred, his eyes
wide open, tinged by the sunrise.

The hour of reverie when the elm
is lit with gold. The day begins.
Think of Max in another realm
too remote for touch, wandering in
a garden. Think of his dark eyeball
surveying darkness for us all.

Now the grave must be
refilled with the full weight of Max.
Beyond the sky's blue filigree,
you cannot see the zodiac
when with sunlight in the air
you cover up his final stare.

Notes to the Cold

The skies crumble like marl, and winter
makes fossils of trees. The light
is vault-gray. By a window a boy
plays his trumpet, high A's and C's
like yellow flowers blown inside out
in a fierce wind. He wipes the spittle off
his mouthpiece and watches knotted sparrows
in nets of snow settle on a white scrim.
Then, as if his great aloneness could be
lofted through the searing gray continuum,
he serenades the snow, the cold blossom
of his trumpet, forever cold, slipping petal
after invisible petal through the window
and the sill. By every trick of light
they are invisible, like the carved initials
of his name encased in snow, but he shows
no sign of stopping, any more than birds
quit ramming their feathery heads
against the snow. And when he does stop,
all is as it was, or seems, unless the boy
is changed. He might be thinking of his father's
words meant as a challenge but not unkindly:
You quit and someone will take over.
He might have hoped one more note
would have emptied the sky of its last snow.
He puts the trumpet in its matter-
of-fact case—there again are his initials—
and walks to the window bluish with snow.
His breath makes a page where, preoccupied,
he draws a bird, fixing the tilt
of its wings so it can fly. Behind it
the black trees struggle in the wind,
the snow falls; through it he sees what's left
of daylight blossom and fade,
and then the bird is gone.

Ode to the Horseshoe Crab

Dullest of all creatures, the horseshoe crab
crawls with its brethren to the beach at low tide;
they are broad-backed with muck-colored plates
and out of water look like stones.

Boys who wouldn't torture anything higher
torture these crabs, which have nothing
that could be called real eyes, their blank backs
suggesting the faces of idiots.

They have no enthusiasms, and can't move fast.
Their undersides are full of twiddling legs
and leaflike gills. *Limulus polyphemus*
has a low sex drive.

Commonly, boys crack the crabs with stones,
large ones that the back can't bear,
and something that looks like brains,
a gray tapioca that smells sweet, comes out.

Having no capacity for love or thought,
they trudge in the salty tide, swallowing small forms
of marine life. In 350 million years the sun
has failed to break their sleep, their sleep before being born.

Papilio

Collecting is a basic human trait. The great collectors
found the Nabokov Pug, *suvarovius* flying by the hundreds,
and the common glider, then spread their wings, medicating them
so carefully that no corruption invaded; they placed
them in beautifully carved bureaus to remember
the graceful madnesses of their flight over the white clearings,
the dark green ferns, the wildflowers, and the peculiar, crooked
        branches
of the thorn apple like crucifixions. Some lay their eggs near violets;
some need the salts and minerals in animal urine;
most are diurnal. The only time I held one in my hand
was when I found it in my garden, fanning itself
on a bean plant. It seemed to have muscles in its wings,
but all I could see, on closer inspection, were its veins, its curled
        proboscis,
and its horrible compound eyes, like those on the fallen preening
        angels
of the imagination. I like to think that its letting me pick it up
was sign of its complicated instinct for survival—in the way its
        eyespots
can persuade birds to peck at a dispensable part of its wings.
When I let it go, it wafted over to the barn wall.
What trick of pen or brush could capture that slightness
of flying? No wonder they are pinned to boards, romantics
        exaggerate
their delicacy, and modern poets dislike them. But they are not frail.
Think of their long thin hearts pumping yellow blood, their
        concealed poisons,
and their pheromones and colors which are sexual—they grow
        transparent
from sex. They are also territorial. Think of the rate of speed of
        autumn.

The Potato Eaters

after Van Gogh

They do not emerge
from the clumsy room
until new light is brought
and they savor morning potatoes.
The sun scours their limbs,
the sparse walls, and furniture.

Naive, they wander outdoors.
The bits of potatoes on the platter
are all that's left of their homely altar.
They go to their work,
superb. To bring them to their senses
we work them to exhaustion

of certain light, uncertain madness.
They feel us breathing
on their backs and hold their collars
as if cold. We barely are aware
of what fright we cause in them.
They offer us potatoes.

Redbirds

The redbirds gathered
in the pines railing the hill
behind the house, the snow grew

colder and empyreal,
and the moon moved into place
in the east. Then

the flock swayed
and was gone, the horizon
crowned by empty iodine.

There were animal tracks
knee-deep, dark troughs
of snow to follow,

and sounds of wind, night's feints
white and stinging
in the rack of winter boughs.

As long as I walked in the absence
of the redbirds, my eyes attuned
to such vague cages

of light as were, shadows took
the shape of Yeti
or winter lion,

frightening beyond sense,
but all the time going away.
I tried to look past

the dense dark,
beyond the close,
beyond whatever closes

when redbirds plunge off the crest
of a hill, but saw only
the chilly reaches of snow.

Who shall say
when I reach the crest of the hill,
the shadows will not be deep

and gray as now
and the world
not have an exit

but a farther field
waning west,
the winds off that snow

cold as fence wire, and no harp?

The Salt Lesson

Looking inside the bony plate, perceive
the gray sponge matter that from its depth
breeds without moving.
Colors belong to the surface, reckon
with the wind mounting tidal waves,
clouds' cover, or a ripple of sun.

Underneath, the seeping calculation,
the dark crevasses and only spots of artificial light.
What the mind allows, sucks
without bloat. Unearthly life,
a grouper eats a man whole; the gold
doubloons; something precious,

spontaneous. The gull returns to the sea
food broken down by sharks.
The mind is a sullen scavenger
with the belly and bowels of a god.

Water city, this impure taker
returns so little, a bubble of stupidity,
a salt piece of itself, of what it endures.

The Snake Skins

The intrigue of this house
is a snake in the foundation, disturbed once
out of his stone place
by a laborer who was removing part of the floor

and southern wall, its lath and crumbling plaster,
to add a sliding glass door.
There were five or six shed skins,
like a multiplication

of the snake's slithering
so close beneath the whispers the night
provoked us to hear and our bare feet.
Now, though more variance of light

pours into the century-old house, flux
and equinox,
and though the laborer cut in half the snake,
I think in darkness, deep in the recesses

of air and dust, in edifices
thought solid, of the little motions
going on, breeding snakes that may
and may

not be meek. I only know
of the spotted adder dead long ago
and these skins like gloves for individual fingers.
I suspect there are others.

Sunfish

Vertebrate, kin to the fully armed form
sprung upon the earth like Athena
from the head of Zeus, how is it no love

or scruples are stirred as you flap
at the end of my line, foul-hooked,
glistening? I recapitulate your gill slits

yet can't make of the life history of fish
a lesson, someone's first flounder
resurrected from a shallow grave,

water sparkling with green points of reflection
like tiny mirrors when green fry
swim out of their scales in fright.

There are no inhibitions, moments of hesitation,
no book of pain borne in your mind
when crawfish with lines tied to them

appear in the pond, and your muscleless face
is a mask the angler cannot pity.
I have held you—spinous, slimy,

and fragrant as dead leaves—in my bare hands
to admire your aegis of blue-green
and yellows shading into one another

as if formed by sunbeams through a shower,
and moments later pulled out your air bladder
with the hook. So naturally was death wrought,

I felt no evil, and so glorious the colors
lying on the surface of the water
robbed of moral.

To Kill a Deer

Into the changes of autumn brush
the doe walked, and the hide, head, and ears
were the tinsel browns. They made her.
I could not see her. She reappeared, stuffed with apples,
and I shot her. Into the pines she ran,
and I ran after. I might have lost her,
seeing no sign of blood or scuffle,
but felt myself part of the woods,
a woman with a doe's ears, and heard her
dying, counted her last breaths like a song
of dying, and found her dying.
I shot her again because her lungs rattled like castanets,
then poked her with the gun barrel
because her eyes were dusty and unreal.
I opened her belly and pushed the insides
like rotted fruit into a rabbit hole,
skinned her, broke her leg joints under my knee,
took the meat, smelled the half-digested smell
that was herself. Ah, I closed her eyes.
I left her refolded in some briars
with the last sun on her head
like a benediction, head tilted on its axis
of neck and barren bone; head bent
wordless over a death, though I heard
the night wind blowing through her fur,
heard riot in the emptied head.

The Tumored Angel

The wings whir more slowly,
weary of holding him halfway between alabastrine
vacancy and a pile of hills. He thumps down hard,
humming a saraband
he's been taught for materializing. His body's
in a sheet, no scrotum, no shoes.
Docile and radiant, he peers
into a trailer window at television
noise and the blue light, at people hiding,
it seems to him, from the cold glory
of fall's sunrise. They're looking at a soap opera.

It's the same story.
The angel is supposed to touch one of them
on the shoulder, these amateur believers,
and in a moment of recognition, like knowing the yelp of hounds
is geese, he or she will sense God's
mastery. This angel doesn't like
easy conversions; he, too, was a man
fluttering toward salvation, as a moth flutters
toward bright lights and destruction.

He changes from veil to flesh
and indicates the tumored hollows of himself
with the sign of the cross. If the believer
reaches in and touches gold, the promised
Paradise, as surely as lights go out, will disappear;
but feeling tumor, he will be reminded of all
the places, drawn quivering and cold,
that cannot be called good unless
someone reaches in and touches and is moved.

The angel squirms when touched (another ploy?)
and thinks of monks in hell; he pictures his insides
as lumps of dead roe and Time burning in coal
blue day. But in his face the heart's color comes,
in his earth-brown eyes the world.
Then he passes without word
through the diminishing sculptures of trees.
The smell of cold leaves scarcely names the event,
and the angel, knowing he is deathless, pauses
before the long climb zenithward, wanting to feel
upon his shoulders not wings, but the weight of the wind.

The Undressing

They took off their clothes 1000 nights
and felt the plaster of the moon
sift over them, and the ground roll
them in its dream. Little did they know
the light and clay and their own sweat
became a skin they couldn't wash away.
Each night bonded to the next,
and they grew stiffer. They noticed this
in sunlight—there were calluses,
round tough moons on their extremities,
shadows under their eyes,
and sometimes a faint sour smell they hadn't had as children.
It worried them, but at night the animal
in their bodies overcame their reluctance
to be naked with each other,
and the mineral moon did its work.
At last when they woke up and were dead,
statues on their backs in the park,
they opened their mouths
and crawled out, pitifully soft and small,
not yet souls.

Untitled

Remember the days of our arguing—
tempests, you called them, your tone wry, mocking;

so disruptive to our physical passion,
and enhancing. Our words struck to the marrow. When,

when, and whenever lust became love was the question.
The room we met in

was like an unforecasted island. Didn't you feel lost
in a way, and afraid? I tasted our sweat as it washed

over us and felt us moving toward our earliest natures—
what the bone frame (ribs and hips) is made for.

In an arboreal mist we knew the fever of the marrow,
greed churning and churning until it lets the other go.

We were alone and there were no appropriate words
afterward

or before.

Venus & Don Juan

She laid her forehead damp with salty water deep in the warmth of
　　his wet chest, and he held her.
After all the ones to which they'd given themselves—that the fates
　　seemed to choose—
there was this. In their affliction they spoke only of their own slow
　　sweet moments in former days,
to tantalize and tear; or of all those others' hands, softskin, genitals;
　　still relying on the senses, still refusing,
until she cried and felt her anger break into pieces so that her shyest
　　places were exposed,
and his heart, which had been growing colder from the cold draught
　　each day brought, and clearer,
clouded over and began to yield. Finding the other willing, and
　　neglecting what those nearest would think,
they lovingly went forth and lost themselves:—once again pain and
　　wildness, again the universe.
Later it would be said: Jealousy overcame them, snaring them in its
　　net, laughing, piercing his side,
his slimness; lamentation to follow. But hadn't they rehearsed,
the pale moon slipping out of the sky each morning, doors shutting,
　　the bedclothes smoothed dry?
And what is left of their story but a fragment and the whispered
　　expressions at midnight
of unheard ghosts who, with their own hearts in turmoil, have not
　　wanted even this much told?

Web-Making

A spider sways along that wondrous slur,
its own silk, thrown from columbine to undiscovered
columbine, and when the cat's moony head
destroys the suspension, the spider
levitates to another flower to loop, in the quiet,
something like a line drawing of a constellation,
botanical, feeling with its 8 legs
for the tensile strength, as the mind plays with theorems.

Sometimes the spider, small as a fingertip, as a star beyond one's
        finger,
on its silk swing swings up high
and winks away.

To study the spider and its web-making
you need a random sample of many
and a delicate telescope to watch the garden, the columbine.
They habitually spin at night.
Dawns you can feel their wet, invisible lines
cross your skin. That's when you notice
the apparent chasms they must cross, and think the natural world
and the quantum heaves of crab, ram & bear
are as the Ancients saw them in the mind's eye,
pulled most delicately
together by silk inventions. What is a web?

Something time takes to finish, or to break,
or to become the way things look in.

Wild Partridge

The same bird over and over again,
quiet so long I had passed by,
drums from the last crisped leaves

up through the branches that had been fire.
Treading moss and stopping my breath,
I've gotten as close as to the russet brink

of an autumn sky and lost it
to the disheveled light . . .
a few wood berries, barley seed

under some pine, a liquid chuckling
somewhere ahead, then on the northern air—
beauty, autumn, vision burning

their overlapping images into dusk.
Can I stalk the wild partridge
and forget, seeing the fallen ash,

the leaves scattered and rotting,
how each moment soars, in truth,
in mortal surprise, away from us always?

Winter Poem

Far past the broken wall, slashed stumps,
homeward or homeless, the black birds
in long purple streaking cling
to the undefinable bulge of the world.

And again I am in winter,
walking across the bronzed marshes
where as a child I went alone to skate.

The branches and hedges held a strange transparency,
as though, at the fall of leaf,
a wall of green twilight reared against them;
and the pond accrued a green and stony glow.

The log on the edge of the pond,
the snow-covered rocks, and the frightened birds
seemed as much laden with deep breath as myself—

the soft thudding sound as I tromped
through the green twilight and the snow
enriched with deer-fall, quill, the sunk solids
of the earthbound.

        I skated easily,
a part of winter, unknowing, like Brueghel's skaters,
black comedians who seem in their blackness

to be keeping watch over the whiteness of space;
like magpies; all of us dipping our wings
in the green twilight, verging
on the vacancy in which we have no place.

Winter Without Snow

The man carried bucket after bucket of plaster dust
up the earthen ramp of the barn that caught fire
and emptied each as if he were dumping snow
onto the blackened beams.
In the trees there were little glass seeds,
souvenirs of winter without snow,

When the man turned back toward the house,
he wore a helmet of dusty mother-of-pearl
and his eyelashes were silvery half-moons.
I watched him with all the coldness I had,
yet it would not snow.

Nothing could make it snow.
Not the burst water pipes, the leggings,
the sleds, or the white horses.
Not the smoky fountains, the clouds.
They were souvenirs of winter without snow,
as was my wish for a white field
like a fresh beginning.